WITHDRAWN

ROBOTICS

FROM CONCEPT TO CONSUMER

BY WIL MARA

CHILDREN'S PRESS®

An Imprint of Scholastic Inc.
New York Toronto London Auckland Sydney
Mexico City New Delhi Hong Kong
Danbury, Connecticut

CONTENT CONSULTANT
Paulo Younse, Engineer, NASA Jet Propulsion Laboratory, Robotic Vehicles and Manipulators
Group, Pasadena, California

PHOTOGRAPHS ©: AFP Photo/HO/Daegu Metropolitan Office of Education: 23; age fotostock:
47, 55 (Javier Larrea), 56 (Lighthouse\UIG); American Honda Motor Co., Inc: 19; AP Images:
26 (Eric Risberg), 15 top (Jens Meyer), 38 (Matt Rourke), 16 (NASA), 48 right, 49 left
(Patricia McDonnell), 11 right (Ted S. Warren); Courtesy of Boston Dynamics/LS3 Robot
image: 25 right; Computer History Museum/Mark Richards: 17; Everett Collection/Mirrorpix:
10 right, 11 left; Festo AG & Co. KG: 24 right, 25 left; Getty Images: 52 left (Education
Images/UIG), 4 left, 12, 15 bottom (Gamma-Keystone), 36 left (Kurita Kaku/Gamma-Rapho),
44 (Matt Cardy), 48 left (Matthew J. Lee/The Boston Globe), 53 top (Pierre Andrieu/AFP),
28 left (Sovfoto/UIG), 58 bottom, 59 left (Toru Yamanaka/AFP); iStockphoto/alexsalcedo:
37; Landov: 3, 5 left, 34, 43 (Ina Fassbender/Reuters), 30 (Kyodo), 46 (Mark/EPA), 22,
35 (Reuters), 58 top (Su Qing/Xinhua), 24 left (Tyrone Siu/Reuters), 6 (Wolfgang Rattay/
Reuters); Media Bakery: 39 (David Leahy), 5 right, 42, 54 (Javier Larrea), 10 left (Joe Fox),
32 (Jon Feingersh), cover (Mark Stevenson); NASA: 52 right, 53 bottom (Goddard Space
Flight Center), 28 right, 29 left, 50 (JPL-Caltech), 29 right (JPL-Caltech/MSSS); Newscom/
Ingram Publishing: 51; Paulo Younse: 40 (Mette Eide), 41; Polaris Images/Adam Nadel: 49
right; Rex USA : 36 right (Barry Phillips/Associated Newspapers), 31 (Geoffrey Robinson), 4
right, 20 (Ray Tang); Science Source/Brian Bell: 27; Shutterstock, Inc.: 59 right (Tristan3D),
57 (wellphoto); Superstock, Inc./Pantheon: 9; From the collections of The Henry Ford, copy
and reuse restriction apply: 14 top, 14 bottom; The Image Works: 18 (Brigitte Friedrich/SZ
Photo), 8 (Mary Evans Picture Library), 13 (SSPL).

LIBRARY OF CONGRESS CATALOGING-IN-PUBLICATION DATA
Mara, Wil, author.
  Robotics : from concept to consumer / by Wil Mara.
    pages cm. — (Calling all innovators: a career for you)
  Summary: "Learn about the history of robotics and find out what it takes to make it in this
exciting career field" — Provided by publisher.
  Audience: Age 9–12.
  Audience: Grades 4–6.
  Includes bibliographical references and index.
  ISBN 978-0-531-20540-2 (library binding) — ISBN 978-0-531-21237-0 (pbk.)
1. Robotics — Juvenile literature. 2. Robotics — History — Juvenile literature. 3. Robotics —
Technological innovations — Juvenile literature. 4. Robotics — Vocational guidance — Juvenile
literature. I. Title.
  TJ211.2.M358 2015
  629.8'92023 — dc23   2014030286

All rights reserved. Published in 2015 by Children's Press, an imprint of Scholastic Inc.
Printed in the United States of America 113

 2 3 4 5 6 7 8 9 10 R 24 23 22 21 20 19 18 17 16 15

Science, technology, engineering, arts, and math are the fields that drive innovation. Whether they are finding ways to make our lives easier or developing the latest entertainment, the people who work in these fields are changing the world for the better. Do you have what it takes to join the ranks of today's greatest innovators? Read on to discover whether robotics is a career for you.

TABLE *of* CONTENTS

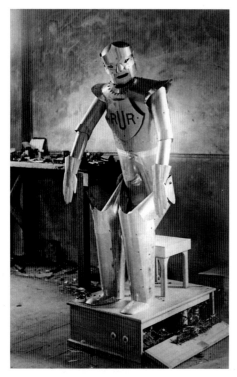

Eric was one of the first robots designed to look and move like a human.

Robosapien has become a popular toy in recent years.

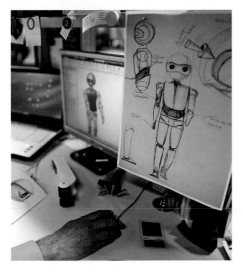

A designer works on ideas for a robot's visual style.

Engineers make adjustments to a robot prototype.

Many of today's
most advanced
robots can move and
behave like humans.

1

THE STUFF OF DREAMS

For thousands of years, humans have dreamed of creating robots that can move and think as if they were living beings. Such machines could be used to perform any number of tasks that are time-consuming, unpleasant, or even impossible for humans to do. This thought has tremendous appeal. By assigning robots to these jobs, people would have more time to do the things they would prefer to do. They would also be kept safe from certain dangerous jobs. This futuristic idea of a robot-powered world is rapidly turning into reality. Robots are becoming more and more common in everyday life. But there was a time when they were merely the stuff of dreams.

ROBOT PIONEERS

1801	1899	1954	1961
Joseph Jacquard builds one of the first programmable robotic devices—an automated loom.	Nikola Tesla builds the world's first remote-control vehicle.	George Devol and Joseph Engelberger design the first workable robotic arm.	The Unimate becomes the first robotic device to be used in a factory.

JUST IMAGINE IT

Thousands of years ago, the ancient Greeks told tales of robotlike creations. One of the most famous examples is the story of Pygmalion. In this tale, Pygmalion carves an ivory sculpture of a woman and falls in love with it. Aphrodite, the Greek goddess of love, brings the statue to life. In another story, the character Hephaestus creates living beings out of metal. While these ancient tales are the product of fantasy, they show the early desire of humans to create beings that could fulfill their wishes.

Even in ancient times, there were a few bold minds that explored the idea of bringing these fantasies to life. The Greek inventor, Hero of Alexandria, is thought to have built a machine that **simulated** human speech.

The story of Pygmalion has inspired plays, paintings, films, and other creative works.

Jacques de Vaucanson's Digesting Duck was much more complex than other robots of the time.

FROM SOLDIERS TO . . . DUCKS?

In the late 1100s and early 1200s, Muslim inventor Al-Jazari constructed a variety of machines called **automatons**. One of these devices served drinks to people. Another handed out soap and small towels when people wanted to wash their hands. In the 1400s, artist and inventor Leonardo da Vinci made detailed plans for a robotic soldier to take the place of humans in battle. However, there is no evidence that he ever built a working model.

In the early 1700s, French inventor Jacques de Vaucanson made some of the most lifelike robots of that time. In 1737, de Vaucanson built a robot capable of playing both the drum and the flute. Another of his creations was known as the Digesting Duck. It could eat and drink as well as flap its wings. The wings alone had more than 400 parts.

THE JOYSTICK

The development of remote-control technology in the latter half of the 1800s played a critical role in the advancement of robotics during the following century. Remote controls use radio waves to send signals from a controller to a machine. This allows people to operate robots and other devices from a distance.

You may have used a joystick to play video games.

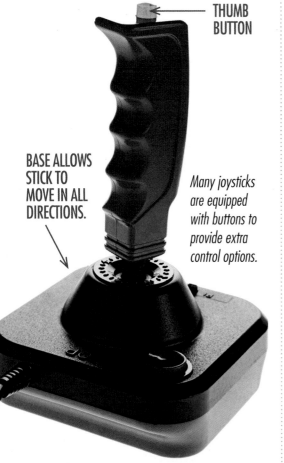

THUMB BUTTON

BASE ALLOWS STICK TO MOVE IN ALL DIRECTIONS.

Many joysticks are equipped with buttons to provide extra control options.

One of the most common devices used to control robots remotely is the joystick. A joystick is a control device that can be gripped and moved around with one hand. It is attached to a circular base and can be tilted in all directions. Many joysticks also have buttons for additional controls. The joystick offers the simplest, most accurate way to control many devices remotely.

PLAYTIME

In the late 1960s, video game pioneer Ralph Baer incorporated joysticks into some of the earliest home game systems. These versatile control devices also made their way into many arcade game machines around the same time. Since then, joysticks have remained one of the most widely used devices for controlling video games. Most modern game controllers use small joysticks that can be operated with just a thumb, rather than requiring a whole hand. ✳

A robot operator uses a joystick to control a dinosaur robot used in live stage performances.

FLYING FROM A DISTANCE

The first remote-control devices were weapons such as missiles and torpedoes. Joysticks enabled operators to carefully guide these explosive weapons through air or water with great accuracy. The first joystick resembling those we know today was developed in the 1920s by engineers at the U.S. Naval Research Laboratory. Joysticks have also been used to pilot a variety of aircraft and spacecraft.

Eric on display in England in 1928

THE HUMAN TOUCH

By the 1920s and 1930s, interest in **humanoid** robots was spreading quickly. Robots were beginning to show up in books and movies with increasing frequency. This spurred the public's imagination and challenged engineers to design real robots that could match the fantasy ones.

Around this time, an English mechanical whiz named William H. Richards built a humanoid robot named Eric. Eric looked quite a bit like the famous Tin Man from *The Wizard of Oz*. Richards brought his creation to the 1928 Exhibition of the Society of Model Engineers in London. During Richards's presentation, Eric rose from a sitting position on a small bench and bowed to the audience. He then looked to his left and right, and spoke to the crowd through a small speaker in his mouth. While the attendees were delighted, there were many people who questioned the value of such a device.

ISAAC ASIMOV

Isaac Asimov is considered one of the greatest science-fiction writers of all time. Asimov considered robots a serious topic and often wrote about the ways he expected them to affect society. His "Three Laws of Robotics" were first mentioned in a short story in 1942 and are still considered relevant today. They are as follows:

1. A robot may not injure a human being or, through inaction, allow a human being to come to harm.
2. A robot must obey the orders given to it by human beings, except where such orders would conflict with the First Law.
3. A robot must protect its own existence as long as such protection does not conflict with the First or Second Law.

FROM WHIMSICAL TO PRACTICAL

By the mid-1900s, many engineers were committing their efforts to creating robots that could do more than simply amuse and entertain. With rapid developments in computer technology, some believed it was possible to design robots that could serve humans in more practical ways. British scientist William Grey Walter began exploring ways to make robotic devices think for themselves. He hoped to create an electronic brain capable of responding to situations in the same way a human might.

In the late 1940s, Walter built robots that showed signs of independent thought. Their slow speed and hard outer shells earned them the nickname "turtles." Nevertheless, by the 1950s there was a growing interest in the scientific community over the question of whether robots really could think on their own. In 1956, the term *artificial intelligence* (AI) was coined during a meeting of robotics experts at Dartmouth College. The study of artificial intelligence would grow to become one of the driving forces in robotics innovation over the following decades.

William Grey Walter built several versions of his "turtle" robots.

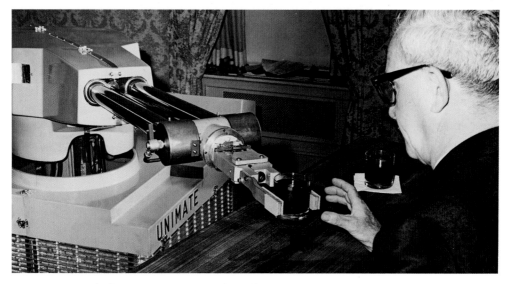

Unimate serves a drink to inventor George Devol.

THE UNIMATE

For many years, people wondered whether a robot could be built to perform tasks on an industrial scale. American inventor George Devol put these questions to rest when he created the Unimate. This groundbreaking device used a robotic arm to perform factory work. The first Unimate machine was sold in 1960 to General Motors. The company put its new robot to work the following year.

AN INCREDIBLE INVENTOR

Born in Kentucky in 1912, Devol had a lifelong interest in all things electrical and mechanical. After high school, he started his own company, United Cinephone, and eventually invented the first electric door, a device that is now commonly seen in buildings everywhere. He first came up with the idea of automated manufacturing in the 1940s and applied for the first related **patent** in 1954.

The first Unimate was used in a General Motors automobile factory.

SAFETY AND SPEED

While the Unimate was not what you might call a big thinker in terms of artificial intelligence, it was able to undertake chores that were considered dangerous to humans. Specifically, it was used to assemble pieces of cars at an automobile assembly plant. This job had previously caused many injuries to human laborers, who had suffered everything from exhaust inhalation to the loss of limbs. Further, the Unimate could work around the clock without so much as a lunch or coffee break. This greatly increased the productivity levels of the factory.

Shortly after the Unimate proved a success for General Motors, other companies began placing orders for

Today, robotic arms play a major role in many types of manufacturing.

Unimates of their own. Over time, robots became more and more common in many types of factories. Today, some factories are almost completely automated, with very few human workers at all. ☀

A Unimate arm pours a cup of tea in a demonstration of its abilities.

CLAW CAN GRIP A VARIETY OF OBJECTS

ROTATING "WRIST" ALLOWS CLAW TO MAKE PRECISE MOVEMENTS

ROBOTS IN SPACE

During the 1960s and 1970s, a strong interest in space exploration swept across the United States. Scientists and engineers began developing ideas for robots that could aid in the exploration of distant planets and moons.

In 1977, the United States' **probes** *Voyager 1* and *Voyager 2* were launched. With no humans aboard, the craft were sent on a mission to explore the outermost planets in our solar system. In the 1980s, the two began sending back groundbreaking data from their journey. In 1986, probes from several different nations were sent to study Halley's comet, which only passes Earth once every 75 to 76 years. Since then, probes have played a major role in space exploration.

The *Voyager 2 spacecraft traveled to distant worlds to gather data about the solar system.*

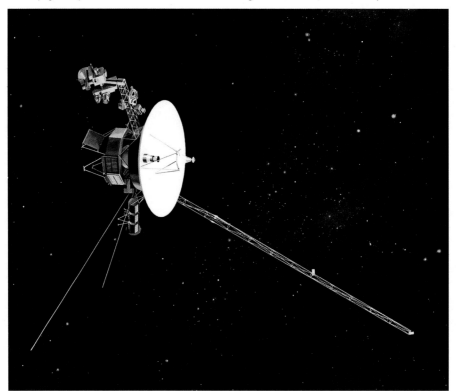

The Stanford Arm had a much wider range of movement than earlier robotic arms.

A NEW TYPE OF WORKER

By the 1970s, robots had taken over numerous jobs that had previously been occupied by people. Most of these jobs were considered dangerous. This made robotic workers a welcome substitution from a safety standpoint. However, it wasn't long before people began questioning the dangers of becoming too "roboticized." While a robot performing a dangerous job meant that there was one less worker at risk, it also left the worker without a job. Some workers could move into safer positions, but others were not so lucky. And what would happen to the workforce if robotic devices were installed in positions that weren't quite so dangerous?

VICTOR SCHEINMAN

In the 1950s, while he was still a high school student, inventor Victor Scheinman designed a machine that could turn speech into text. The following decade, while attending Stanford University, he invented a computer-controlled robotic arm that could move in more directions than any previous robotic arm. Known as the Stanford Arm, it revolutionized the robotics industry by making robots better than ever at manufacturing jobs.

Scientist and writer Joseph Weizenbaum cautioned against putting too much faith in artificial intelligence.

THE ETHICAL QUESTION

Company leaders delighted at the prospect of more robotic laborers. These new workers wouldn't need medical benefits. They wouldn't call in sick or need weekends or holidays off. People who relied on jobs that could be filled by robots became increasingly nervous. Factory workers were especially aware that they could be replaced at their jobs. At some companies, entire departments were producing goods with minimal aid from human workers. Technology soon reached a point where robotic workers could produce goods even faster than human workers could.

In 1976, as artificial intelligence and robotic performance were rapidly advancing, computer scientist Joseph Weizenbaum published the landmark book *Computer Power and Human Reason: From Judgment to Calculation*. Weizenbaum made powerful arguments against relying too heavily on artificial intelligence. He argued that robots, no matter how advanced, were only capable of calculation and choice. They lacked the benefit of critical human elements such as morality and experience. Weizenbaum's book sparked a debate about the ultimate role robots should play in our society. Conversation surrounding this controversial issue rages on to this day.

FORGING AHEAD

Since the 1980s, robotic development moved at a fairly rapid pace. In 1984, a robot called WABOT-2 was unveiled. WABOT-2 possessed 10 fingers and 2 feet. It was capable of playing the organ and reading complex sheet music. Within a few years, robots that could smoothly interact with people were being produced relatively inexpensively. By the end of the decade, the groundwork was laid for the creation of Deep Blue. This computer was so good at chess that it defeated the highest-ranked human player in the world in 1997.

During the 1990s, Honda revealed its P-series humanoid robots. The company took a further step in 2000 with its ASIMO robot. ASIMO looked more like a person inside a spacesuit than someone you'd see on the street. Nevertheless, it was able to carry on a conversation and recognize people it had seen before. It could also walk, run, and pick up or carry objects. It wasn't quite C-3PO from *Star Wars*, but it wasn't too far off either.

FLEXIBLE JOINTS ALLOW ASIMO TO MOVE LIKE A HUMAN

ASIMO demonstrates some of its physical abilities by kicking a ball.

Robotics scientist Mark Tilden poses with Robosapien, a popular robotic toy he invented.

2

THAT WAS THEN, THIS IS NOW

Robotics technology has developed at a remarkable speed over the last few decades. The latest and greatest advancements have brought yesterday's science-fiction stories to life. Robots are helping people to achieve things that were once impossible. They are also simplifying everyday activities that were once complex or difficult. However, introducing new types of robots often requires people to make big adjustments to the way they have gotten used to doing things. As robots become smarter and more similar to people, we may find that the biggest difficulty is simply getting used to living side by side with our robotic friends.

PROPOSED FUTURE ROBOTICS PROJECTS

2015	2017	2020	2022
The U.S. Department of Defense plans to employ robots for at least one-third of its on-the-ground military force.	South Korea's government estimates that there will be a robotic device in every home in the nation.	Engineers hope to have nanorobots—robots so small that they are invisible to the naked eye—working in several industries.	Experts hope that about a third of all robots will be able to learn to make intelligent decisions on their own.

THE LUKE SKYWALKER ARM

At the end of the movie *Star Wars: The Empire Strikes Back*, the character Luke Skywalker loses his hand in a battle. A short time later, he receives a new robotic hand that looks and functions almost exactly like a real one. When the movie was released in 1981, this robotic hand was pure science fiction. This might not be the case for much longer.

In May 2014, the Food and Drug Administration (FDA) approved a robotic **prosthetic** arm made by DEKA Integrated Solutions. Known as the Luke arm in honor of the *Star Wars* character, it is one of the most lifelike prosthetics ever built. The device weighs approximately the same as a real arm. It also includes five working fingers that can move and bend almost exactly like those on a real hand. It responds to the muscle movements of an injured person's remaining arm. Unlike older prosthetics, it allows users to perform small, precise movements. For example, people with Luke arms can turn keys in a car ignition, pick up eating utensils, or button a shirt. These tasks are well beyond the limits of other prosthetic devices.

The Luke arm allows users to do almost anything they could do using a real hand.

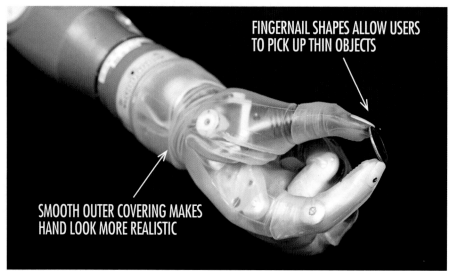

FINGERNAIL SHAPES ALLOW USERS TO PICK UP THIN OBJECTS

SMOOTH OUTER COVERING MAKES HAND LOOK MORE REALISTIC

Korean students learn English from a special teaching robot that can talk and read to them.

BOTS IN THE CLASSROOM

Ever wonder what it would be like to walk into a classroom and see a robot sitting behind the teacher's desk? You might find out someday soon. Robotic devices are rapidly proving themselves to be effective teaching tools. There are already numerous robots that can teach basic subjects such as math, science, and reading in a fun and interactive way. Their development is part of a growing trend toward a robot-based branch of educational technology. Promising results have been seen from younger grades all the way up to the college level.

These devices take many forms, from rolling spheres to full-sized humanoid robots. Some connect wirelessly to tablets or other mobile devices. This allows each student to have a more personalized learning experience. This isn't to say that modern teaching robots are replacing human teachers completely. Instead, they are used as teaching assistants. Students interact with a robot while a human teacher acts as a guide and supervisor. Some of the teaching robots are customizable, so teachers can adjust lesson plans. There are even **drone** robots that can fly around a classroom via remote control.

MODERN MARVEL

Atlas, named after a character in classic mythology who was forced to carry the weight of the sky on his shoulders. It is an appropriate name, because the Atlas robot is designed not to harm, but to help and support. Standing 6 feet (1.8 meters) tall with a humanoid shape, Atlas is programmed to handle a variety of search-and-rescue operations. This includes aiding injured people, driving vehicles, and venturing into places that are unsafe for humans, such as fires or chemical spills. Atlas is equipped with cutting-edge robotic technology, including a laser range finder, powerful limbs, and cameras, all built around a structure of aluminum and titanium.

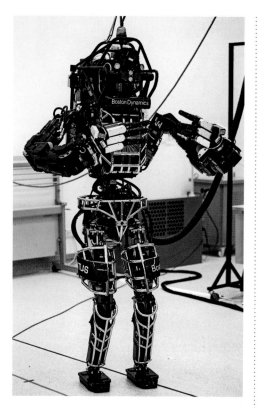

The Atlas robot weighs around 330 pounds (150 kilograms).

ROBOTS IN THE MILITARY

Many of today's most advanced robots are being created to help militaries fight wars while minimizing the loss of human life. While there's been much talk about the military developing robotic soldiers programmed and designed specifically for warfare, we hear a lot less about the robots the military is putting together for other reasons. One of them is known as

A VERY SMART BIRD

The idea of flying robots isn't anything new. Nor is the idea of robots that behave like animals. So what about a robot that's a little of both? This is where a fascinating new robot called the SmartBird comes in. First unveiled in April 2011 in Germany, the SmartBird is modeled after a herring gull. It flies by flapping its mechanical wings. The SmartBird can also make turns, land, and take off again. Most interestingly, the SmartBird travels with very little noise. Because it is so quiet and looks like a real bird, the SmartBird can fly relatively unnoticed. This would make it good at spying on enemies.

LS3 robots use animal-like movements to walk across even the most difficult terrain.

From a distance, SmartBirds look almost like real birds.

GIDDYAP

For several years, the U.S. Department of Defense has been hard at work on a series of robots known as Legged Squad Support Systems (LS3s). These robots look like multi-legged animals. They can operate in harsh conditions and travel across almost any kind of land. Their primary purpose is to carry large, heavy military equipment through areas where vehicles cannot travel. LS3s are primarily meant for military use. They can carry hundreds of pounds of supplies across complex and rugged terrain. They are also designed to follow human leaders and obey spoken commands, just like real soldiers. ✳

SENSORS HELP THE CAR NAVIGATE

Google's new self-driving cars could change the way people travel.

BACKSEAT DRIVERS

Robot-controlled cars are on the way. Several technology companies have been pouring resources into creating automated cars for some time now. Among them is Google, which has made the biggest advancements seen in the field so far.

An automated car cannot operate entirely on its own. It still needs a human being in the driver's seat to help direct it. The driver can decide how much he or she wants to control directly and how much he or she wants to leave to the car's automated system. A typical automated car has an advanced computer and numerous sensors. These systems can carefully monitor more of the car's immediate surroundings than a human ever could. The car also knows the local roadways inside and out thanks to **GPS** and other navigation technology. Similarly, the car is aware of local speed limits and other laws. This can go a long way toward reducing the number of crashes and speeding violations.

ROBOTIC WHEELCHAIRS

Thanks to recent robotic developments, wheelchairs are getting even better at helping people get around. Researchers at the Massachusetts Institute of Technology (MIT) have designed a wheelchair that responds to voice commands. For example, if a user says, "Take me to the kitchen," the wheelchair will begin rolling in that direction. Sensors can detect furniture or other objects and adjust the chair's path accordingly. The chair can remember where such obstacles are located so it can plan faster routes.

Remarkably, the chair's designers have programmed it to respond to less direct commands as well. For example, the chair may bring its user into the dining room following a comment such as "I'd like to have dinner now." If a user is unable to speak aloud, commands can be typed using a keypad.

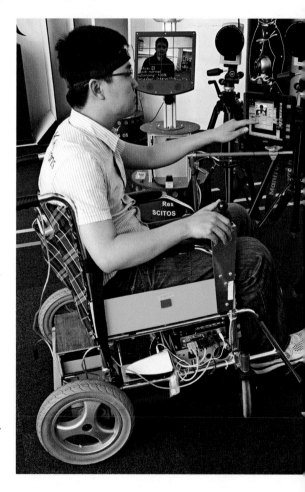

Researchers are working on robotic wheelchairs that can be controlled using small facial movements.

FROM THIS TO THAT

Lunokhod 1 *undergoes testing before its 1970 moon mission.*

REMARKABLE ROVERS

The rover robotic device was designed with the sole purpose of exploring other planets. These incredible robots are transported to distant worlds and travel around on their surfaces. For decades, they have been providing scientists with valuable information about outer space. Today's rovers have undergone significant changes and improvements since the technology's earliest days.

ROBOTS ON THE MOON

The first successful rover was designed for the Soviet Union by Armenian scientist Alexander Kemurdzhian. It was sent to the moon in 1970. Called the *Lunokhod 1*, it landed on the lunar surface on November 17. It was a relatively simple rover by today's standards, equipped with little more than a cone-shaped antenna, four television cameras, and an x-ray device. Operating via remote control, it took numerous photos and analyzed the moon's soil.

REACHING THE RED PLANET

Although the Soviets made several attempts to take the next step in the rover evolution by putting a rover on Mars, the United States was the first to make this breakthrough. In July 1997, the *Sojourner* rover reached the surface of the red planet. *Sojourner* was powered in large part by solar cells. It took hundreds of high-resolution photos, performed chemical analyses on Mars's rocks and soil, and gathered data about the atmosphere.

Engineers pose with several different Mars rovers.

Curiosity is one of the most advanced rovers created so far.

RETURN TO MARS

In 2011, NASA launched the *Curiosity* rover, again with the purpose of exploring the Martian surface. *Curiosity* is the most advanced robotic rover currently in operation. It weighs nearly a ton and is equipped with two onboard computers and multiple communication systems. It also has numerous cameras, a dust-removal device, a microscope, a weather station, and a robotic arm with a scoop and drill to collect samples from the surface. *Curiosity* can sense and avoid dangerous situations, helping to prevent it from being damaged as it explores Mars's rocky surface. ☀

MORE LIFELIKE THAN EVER

The people of Japan may soon find some unfamiliar faces on their television screens when they turn on the news. In June 2014, Japanese robotics whiz Hiroshi Ishiguro unveiled a pair of robots that look and act eerily like real humans. The robots were designed to resemble young women dressed in newscaster outfits. Reporters at the event were allowed to question the androids, and the robots' replies were remarkably realistic. Perhaps even more impressive was the fact that the robots were handed pages of news text, which they read aloud without a hitch.

There were some minor problems. For example, one robot's lips remained still while it spoke, and the other gave no reply when asked a question. But these issues were easily corrected and took nothing away from the clear message that robots that look just like us might soon become a familiar part of society.

One of Hiroshi Ishiguro's lifelike robots was used to offer information to customers at a clothing store in Osaka, Japan.

REALISTIC HAIR AND FACE MAKE THE ROBOT LOOK MORE HUMAN

ROBOTIC ARM ALLOWS THE DALEK TO EXTEND FROM A TRUCK

LIGHT KEEPS PEOPLE OR VEHICLES FROM RUNNING INTO THE DALEK WHILE IT IS WORKING

The Dalek makes fixing potholes a simple process.

A SMOOTH ROAD AHEAD

Potholes are a major nuisance for drivers and cyclists. However, repairing these holes is a lot of work. It can be difficult for workers to keep up with all of the new potholes that form. Robots might be able to solve this problem.

The Dalek is a robotic device developed in England. Named for characters in the television show *Doctor Who*, the Dalek can fix potholes about 30 times faster than people can. This means the Dalek needs only about two minutes to repair each pothole. The Dalek is a robotic arm that can be attached to a truck. A human operator inside the truck uses a computer and a joystick to control the arm's movement. The Dalek blows a jet of air to clear all the loose particles from a pothole. Then it sprays glue that looks much like tar. Next it loads the hole with gravel. Finally, it lays a smooth layer of asphalt over the gravel, levels the area, and leaves the asphalt to dry.

SOLAR PANELS

A high school student demonstrates his solar-powered robot design to a teacher.

3

ON THE JOB

The robotics field has seen significant growth in the past few years. It is likely to continue growing in the years ahead. This growth will provide plenty of opportunities for young engineers and scientists to make their mark on the industry. Students who are interested in robotics should take courses in subjects such as electronics, mechanics, engineering, and computer technology. A college education is required for almost any job in the robotics field. Many jobs might even require advanced degrees. However, more schools are offering robotics-related courses than ever before. This means there are plenty of options available to young people who would like to create tomorrow's most incredible robots.

NUMBER OF INDUSTRIAL ROBOTS IN USE

1990	1995	2000	2010	2015
40,000	70,000	95,000	120,000	180,000 (projected)

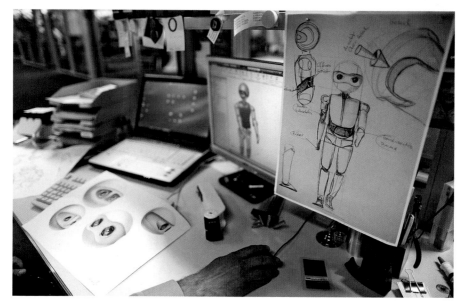

Engineers might sketch out many different designs before making a final choice.

THE ENGINEER

One of the most important jobs in the world of robots is that of robotics engineer. Put very simply, a robotics engineer is involved in every aspect of the creation of a robot. He or she follows the project from its planning and design to construction and final testing.

In the past, early stages of a robotics engineer's work involved sketching ideas with a pencil and paper, then cobbling together models to watch how they worked. These days, most robotics engineers can complete these planning and design stages using computer simulations. Once the main idea of a new robot has been decided, the robot is "assembled" on screen and put through simulated tests. This computer-based approach keeps down costs of materials and labor. It also makes it easy for engineers to experiment with a robot's design. Creating new and unproven robots can require a lot of trial and error. Good engineers have realistic expectations and plenty of patience.

BUILDING AND LEARNING

Once a robot seems to be working correctly on screen, the engineer oversees construction of a **prototype**. There are usually more problems to solve after the prototype is done. Computer simulations work well, but they're still far from perfect. Issues that the simulation didn't catch might pop up once a real robot is put into action. The engineer thinks of ways to solve these problems.

Robotics engineers are almost always expected to have a bachelor's degree. In college, they mainly study subjects such as electronics, mechanics, and computers. Even after graduating from college, robotics engineers are expected to keep learning. They stay up-to-date with the latest advances in technology. This helps give them new ideas for their projects and keeps them competitive with other engineers.

A Ugandan robotics engineer tests a robot designed to disarm bombs.

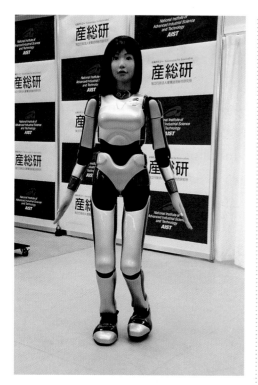

Artists and designers work together to make humanoid robots look as lifelike as possible.

HAIR AND MAKEUP?

A big part of creating new robots is deciding how they will look. Designing their appearance has become a complex process. In recent years, robotics expert Hiroshi Ishiguro has been working on a series of robots called Geminoids. They look so much like humans that many people have trouble telling them apart from humans at first sight. Everything from facial features to hair color, style, and texture are carefully designed. This represents a colossal step in android design and a triumph of robotic artistry. The hope is that the Geminoids will become lifelike enough to make actual humans feel comfortable in their presence, opening new possibilities for human-robot interaction in fields such as education.

WILD KINGDOM

While some creators are making robots that look more and more human, others are trying to imitate the look of animals. There is a little robot called the hexapod, for example, that looks like a very large insect. It has six legs and can crawl over difficult

Hexapod robots were inspired by the movements of animals such as insects.

A hexacopter's design makes it lightweight and maneuverable.

terrain while carrying a variety of objects. While insects are not generally known for helping people carry things, the main idea of this kind of robot design is to imitate an animal's natural features to create a useful robot. This process is known as biomimicry. With millions of different animals to serve as inspiration, future robot designers will have a lot to work with.

LET'S BE PRACTICAL

There are some robots that don't look or act like humans or animals at all. Many do their jobs alone and out of sight. While a robot intended to interact with children needs a friendly, inviting appearance, one designed to vacuum a pool simply needs to do its job as effectively as possible. The same is true of the hexacopter—a flying robot with laser-based radar that enables it to record 3D images of its surroundings. The robot's equipment is mounted on a circular device with six posts sticking out of it. There is a spinning blade at the end of each post. It might not look very interesting, but its shape allows it to get the job done. Sometimes looks aren't the most important part of designing a robot's shape. ✳

THE TECHNICIAN

Machines break down no matter how well they're built. This is true of even the most advanced robots. As the world becomes filled with more and more robots, there will be a growing need for people who know how to fix them. For those who have a knack for mechanics and are good with computers, becoming a robot technician could be a very good career choice.

Remember that robots are made up of two parts—hardware and software. This means robot technicians are more than just mechanics. They must also be able to solve problems with the computer programs that make a robot work. Many of these programs are specially made for specific robots. That means robot technicians must be able to quickly learn a variety of new programs as needed.

A technician works on a manufacturing robot in a Pennsylvania factory.

ROBOT CONTROLLED REMOTELY
VIA LAPTOP COMPUTER

Some robots operated entirely by remote control, with every move being determined by an operator.

THE OPERATOR

Now you know about the people who build robotic devices and the people who repair and maintain them. But what about the people who actually use them? These workers are called robotic machine operators. The simplest way to think of them is as the folks who work a robot's controls. Because there are so many types of robotic devices being used these days, each operator needs a unique set of skills and training.

In a manufacturing setting, a robot might assemble a product. However, a human operator may be required to load up the robot with the raw materials it needs to do the assembling. The operator might also need to monitor the robot at all times to make sure it's working properly. He or she may need to adjust the robot's settings to keep things running smoothly.

Some robots might require different attachments to complete different tasks. For example, a robot that drills holes might need different drill bits for different holes. An operator needs to change these parts to fit the job. Similarly, certain robot parts might become dull or worn down with use. It is the operator's responsibility to replace these parts as needed.

Paulo Younse is a member of the Robotic Vehicles and Manipulators Group at the NASA Jet Propulsion Laboratory in Pasadena, California. He has helped to create highly advanced uncrewed robotic vehicles.

When did you start thinking about getting into the field of space exploration? What was it about this discipline that interested or inspired you? When I was 10 years old, I came across a book on astronomy at the bookstore. I curiously opened it up and found my imagination transported throughout the solar system from the pages of pictures and descriptions of the various planets. Learning about the mysteries of our solar system and engineering challenges required to solve these drove me to pursue a career in space exploration.

What kinds of classes did you take in middle school, high school, and beyond in order to prepare for your career? Throughout middle school and high school, science and math classes helped me understand how the universe works, as well as create things that move and interact with the world. English classes helped me write proposals and scientific reports for my job, communicate with other coworkers effectively, and read very fast to keep up with the latest technology published regularly in books, magazines, and scientific journals. Art classes helped me develop the creativity needed to invent new things, think in three-dimensional space to visualize new engineering designs, and make accurate drawings of mechanical parts.

What other projects and jobs did you do in school and your work life before beginning your career? And how did that work prepare you? After college, I got my first engineering job at Boeing helping design and test an underwater robot. This job gave me the opportunity to practice the science, math, and engineering skills I studied in my classes, as well as learn how to be a good engineer from talking and working with the other engineers on the project.

Do you have a particular project that you're especially proud of or that you think really took your work to another level? One of the projects I'm most proud of is the hopping robot I got to develop. It was a prototype of a six-legged robot the size of a basketball designed to explore low-gravity environments like the moon. It was the first project I got to manage while at the Jet Propulsion Lab, and it was an extremely fun and challenging engineering task.

It obviously takes teamwork to make things happen in the field of space exploration. Does working as part of a team come naturally to you, or was it something you had to learn and work on? Building a robot to explore space is extremely complicated and requires the expertise of many people working together as a team. I gained experience working in and leading teams through many different experiences while growing up—from playing on my local soccer team, completing group projects in class, and organizing teams of volunteers after school to helping out at the local homeless shelter and senior center.

What would your dream project be if you were given unlimited resources? If I had unlimited resources, I would love to have the opportunity to design and build a robot that could travel to Jupiter's moon Europa, drive around on the surface, tunnel through the ice, and swim around the potential oceans underneath the ice in search of life!

What advice would you give to a young person who wants to do what you do one day? If you want to pursue a career in space exploration, you need to study hard and get good grades in all your subjects in school—not just science and math, but reading, writing, and art as well. You should also get as much hands-on experience designing, investigating, and building things on your own, such as fixing your bike, constructing things out of wood, building and programming robot kits, and taking apart old machines to learn how they work. ☀

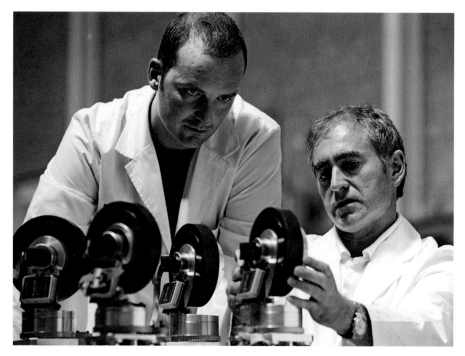
Researchers compare different wheel designs for a robot.

THE RESEARCHER

Robots have come a very long way since people first thought of building machines that perform human functions. However, there is still plenty of room for improvement. This is where the critical field of robotic research comes in. A researcher is someone who studies robots to look for ways to make them better. He or she takes part in the development of new robotic devices. A researcher also spends a lot of time examining robots that are already out in the world performing their assigned functions.

A researcher's job is based on the art of asking the right questions. How can this work faster? How can it perform more efficiently? How can the error rate be reduced? Why does it break down exactly every 14 days? Are there better materials with which to build it? Can it be made more inexpensively? Should it be larger? Smaller? Faster? Slower?

THE PROGRAMMER

Without our brains, our bodies wouldn't be much good. Similarly, a robot without software just sits there gathering dust. It is up to robotics programmers to design the computer software that makes a robot perform tasks. They create this software by writing code in one of many programming languages. The code contains commands that tell the robot how to act in different situations. For example, a robot that performs assembly tasks may reach for an item that is part of the assembly procedure. If the item is not there, the software must then lead the robot to halt its assembly process and issue an alert that more raw materials are needed.

The software that powers robots is often designed from the ground up. Each robot requires a unique program to make it run effectively. Robot programmers therefore need more than just extensive knowledge of programming basics. They must also have the creativity needed to come up with highly original software.

German programmers work on software for a humanoid robot.

A British engineer assembles the pieces of a humanoid robot arm.

4

IT'S ALIVE!

B uilding a new robot is a lot like creating any other piece of technology. The process moves one step at a time. However, there are a lot of steps involved in creating a robot. And as robots become more and more complex, so does the process of making them. The robots become more useful, but it takes more time and money to design, build, and perfect them. The engineers and researchers who design new robots do not have unlimited resources. They have to work with what they have to create the best possible robot. To do this, they must work together, share ideas, and brainstorm solutions to any difficulties that arise. With hard work and a little luck, they might create the next robot that revolutionizes the way we live.

AI ADVANCES

1950	1974	1985	1997	2011
Alan Turing publishes a paper proposing the possibility of AI.	Eliza, the world's first "chatterbot," responds to human questions.	AARON, a program that creates its own artwork, is unveiled.	The Deep Blue chess program defeats world champion chess player Garry Kasparov.	The Watson computer from IBM defeats two champions on the trivia show Jeopardy!

A CASE OF NEED

The first step in the birth of any new robot is to answer a very simple question: What purpose will it serve? All robots must serve a function. This might be something as important as assisting with a complicated surgery. It might also just be something fun, such as serving drinks or playing music. A robot's purpose will determine what features it has, what it looks like, and what it is made of. For example, a robot intended to roll around the surface of Mars will not be designed and built in the same way as a robot that vacuums a swimming pool.

Once a team decides what kind of robot to make, there are other questions to be answered. Let's think about the example of a Mars rover. How long will the robot have to actively function each day? Will it mostly stay still, or will it need to move around a lot? Will it return to Earth after its mission is complete? And what will the robot do when it arrives on Mars? Will it photograph the planet's surface? Pick up rocks? The team must consider all of these questions and more before moving forward with the project.

A robot designed to serve food to restaurant customers requires far different features from one designed to assemble automobiles at a factory.

A team might look at older robots in order to come up with new ideas.

THE DRAWING BOARD

The team must also consider how much it will cost to complete its project and how long it will take. Thanks to years of research and development in robotics, robots are less expensive to produce than ever before. However, that doesn't mean they're cheap. Building another copy of a robot that already exists is a fairly inexpensive undertaking because the developmental work has already been done. But brand-new robots require much more time and labor. This results in a much greater cost.

Once the team knows what the scope and budget of the project will be, it can begin the design work. There really isn't a "right way" to approach the design of a new robot. The people who design robots don't just turn on their imaginations when they arrive at work and then turn them off when they go home. The designers think about the new robot even when they are doing other things. They propose ideas to each other and explore a variety of possible options. Ideas that don't work are set aside. Ideas that do work are expanded and revised. Eventually, a design for the robot begins to take shape.

WHERE THE MAGIC HAPPENS

MIT'S ROBOTICS PROGRAM

The Massachusetts Institute of Technology (MIT) is one of the most respected research institutions in the world. Founded in the mid-1800s in Cambridge, Massachusetts, MIT focuses primarily on science and engineering. It also emphasizes active research into the design and creation of useful technologies. There are numerous robotics labs on the MIT campus, each with its own specific area of focus. One concerns itself with developing movement systems for robots. Another strives for advancements in artificial intelligence. A third is MIT's haptics lab. Haptics is the science of sensing and manipulating objects through direct physical contact.

MIT graduate James McLurkin poses with his award-winning SwarmBots.

An MIT student uses a remote control to operate a "skiing" robot he created.

PAST AND PRESENT SUCCESSES

MIT teams have made significant advances in everything from the design of prosthetics to the interactions between robots and humans. MIT robots have also contributed to space exploration and medicine. One of MIT's important early creations was Genghis, a six-legged walking robot that demonstrated the possibility of using robots to explore the surface of other planets.

THE BEST AND BRIGHTEST

Many of today's most brilliant robot developers got their start at MIT. Alex Slocum earned his doctorate in 1985 and has since gone on to become one of MIT's engineering professors. He holds more than 100 patents and has developed dozens of high-tech products. Colin Angle and Helen Greiner, who both earned bachelor's degrees at MIT in 1989, went on to form the company iRobot. It produces robots for consumer, industrial, and military uses. James McLurkin, who earned his doctorate in 2008, was the creator of the SwarmBot, a system of many simple robots working together to reach a goal.

Another was the Ant series of robots. These tiny robots could move around and perform a variety of functions using their sensors. More recently, MIT's developers have been working on robots that will assist drivers and reduce the number of road accidents; robots that give household pets exercise and entertainment when owners aren't around; and robots that help children learn.

Students work on projects at MIT's artificial-intelligence lab.

TEXTURE OF WHEELS HELPS
THE ROVER ROLL ON A
VARIETY OF SURFACES

Robot designers and engineers carefully consider the features their creation will need to succeed in its intended environment.

PIECE BY PIECE

Rough sketches are made, discussions take place, and 3D images are drawn on computers. The team makes sure each detail of the robot fits in with its intended purpose. Let's go back to the example of a Mars rover. Such a robot would need wheels in order to roll around the Martian surface. But what kind of wheels would work best? Temperatures are very hot during the day and extremely cold at night on Mars. These sudden changes would cause rubber tires to wear out quickly. Also, there would be no way to change the tires if they go flat. When NASA designed its Mars rovers, its engineers used metal wheels to deal with these issues. However, even these strong wheels get holes in them after driving around Mars's rocky surface for years at a time.

Designers also need to figure out how much human interaction will be required to operate the robot. Then they need to determine how these controls will work. Speech-recognition technology has evolved fairly rapidly in recent years. This enables many robots to respond to voice commands. Other robots must be controlled manually with keypads, touch screens, or joysticks.

PULLING TOGETHER THE PARTS

After a robot's design has been finalized, the next step is to gather what will be needed to build the prototype. This is the very first functioning model of the robot. Working from their sketches and other plans, engineers will gather each piece required for assembly. In some cases these materials may be easy to get. For example, a circuit board or a small motor can be purchased from a supplier. In other cases, the engineers may have to build their own parts from scratch. If a robot needs a metal arm of a specific length and shape, for example, it may have to be molded into a custom shape. The same is true for most of the computer software that drives a robot. It is not unusual for robot designers to work with programmers to create new software.

Custom metal pieces are made by pouring hot liquid metal into a mold and allowing it to cool.

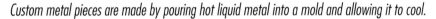

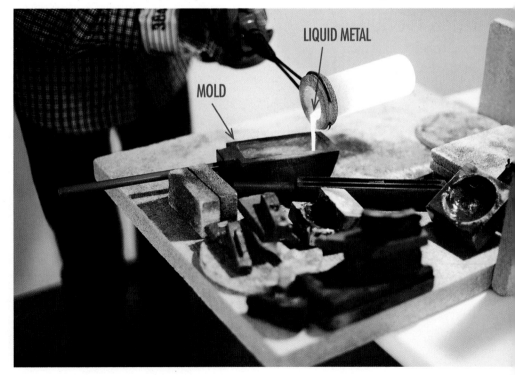

LIQUID METAL

MOLD

LASTING CONTRIBUTIONS

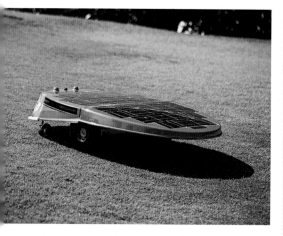

A solar-powered lawn mower robot uses the power of sunlight to keep grass at the right length.

USING THE SUN

Solar panels, which were invented decades ago, are a critical component of many outdoor-functioning robotic devices. While there have been some improvements in their design, their purpose has remained precisely the same—to convert sunshine into usable energy. The key component to a solar panel is the solar cell. A solar cell takes advantage of something called the photovoltaic effect to convert sunlight into electricity.

THROUGH THE YEARS

The first modern photovoltaic cell was presented to the public by Bell Laboratories in 1954. In the late 1950s, solar cells were added to spacecraft. This allowed the craft to go on longer missions by extending battery life. An important turning point came during the 1970s, when a shortage of oil supplies drove companies to begin investing in the development of solar panels, which could replace the need for fossil fuels. In the 1990s, new panels were developed that were much less expensive to produce. Today, the number of homes that use solar panels is at a record high.

This solar-powered robot was invented to eliminate the need for tractors and dangerous chemicals.

Engineering students test solar-powered rover designs at a summer camp sponsored by NASA.

PERFECT FOR ROBOTS

Due to increasing affordability, solar panels have become ideal for use with robots. Robots that have regular exposure to sunlight can use the sun's energy as a primary source of power or to keep their batteries charged. Furthermore, solar panels are generally lighter than batteries, and lighter robots do not need as much energy to run.

Rovers are a good example of solar-powered robots. Modern rovers even have programming that lets them know when their batteries are running low. They can then position themselves so their panels will receive maximum sunlight. Solar power is also an ideal option for robots that perform outdoor chores such as vacuuming pools or mowing lawns. Similarly, solar heat will likely become a power option for automobiles in the near future. ☀

GENERAL ASSEMBLY

Once all the parts are ready, it is time for the engineers to assemble the prototype. They use a variety of tools to connect the robot's many pieces. Other robots might even be required to aid assemblers with particularly delicate or difficult tasks. Robot assembly usually takes place in a clean, well-lit laboratory. Some robots are put together within a scaffolding structure. This is a rigid set of poles and pipes on which the robot can be hung so it won't get damaged.

This also makes it easier for the assemblers to move around or get underneath the robot.

Engineers often continue to make changes to the robot's design as they are building the prototype. They might find that some aspect of the robot doesn't work once it is assembled. They might also notice ways to improve the robot that they hadn't thought of yet.

As a robot nears completion, the team examines and tests individual components to make sure they are installed correctly and functioning properly.

The team takes careful notes as it observes the robot during testing.

PUTTING IT TO THE TEST

Once the robot has been fully assembled, it is time to test it out. Some engineers consider this the most crucial step in the process. If a prototype does not function properly, it may need to be totally redesigned.

The testing process must ensure that a robot can handle everything that it might need to deal with. Engineers usually put a robot through even more than it would endure under normal operating circumstances. That way they know the robot is more than capable of handling its job under everyday conditions.

There are many different types of tests for robots. They all depend on what kind of robot is being built. Robots that travel through space are tested to make sure they can withstand extreme conditions, such as extreme cold or heat. The engineers also perform tests on their communications systems to make sure the robot will be able to stay in touch from millions of miles away.

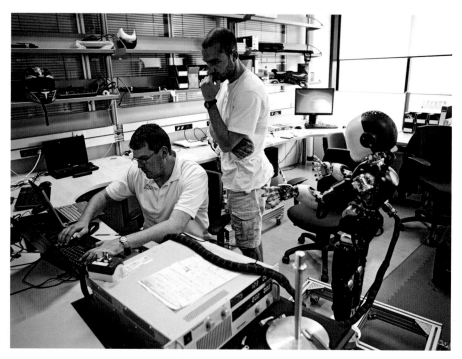
Testing reveals bugs and other issues that need to be resolved before a robot is completed.

WORKING OUT THE KINKS

During the testing process, the engineers observe, measure, and take notes about everything that happens. They search everywhere for signs of weakness in the robot. Again, it all comes down to questions. Did the robot perform the task fast enough? Did the human subject find it easy to input commands? Did the robot respond to situations in the way the programmers hoped?

Although engineers always hope for the best, it is nearly impossible for a robot to sail through testing without any problems. The engineers work to solve every problem that pops up, from the smallest issues to the most major flaws. They test, make adjustments, and then test again until everything works exactly the way they want it to. Testing a new robot can take months or even years. However, the hard work pays off when the robot is finally ready to go.

INTO THE WORLD

With any luck, the robot is soon completed and sent to its intended user. However, the robot's creators are still not finished with their job. They continue to monitor the robot to ensure that it is effective. They also search for improvements that can be made in newer versions of the robot. Some robots send information through the Internet back to the company that produced them. Others are monitored using video cameras. Robot maintenance crews may also pass information back to the robots' makers. Patterns that develop over a long period of time can be studied carefully. This information is useful not only to the company that built the robot but also to tomorrow's engineers. They will look back at the accomplishments of the past and dream up new ways that robots can help make the world a better place. Then the process of creating a new robot will begin all over again!

SUCTION CUPS FOR GRIPPING BOXES

Even after a robot has been put to work, the team continues searching for ways to improve the design.

THE FUTURE

Some farming robots can recognize colors, enabling them to pick only ripe fruit from a plant.

OLD MACDONALD GETS A BREAK

One of the main benefits of robots is that they can perform repetitive tasks that are difficult for humans—and there are few jobs more labor-intensive than farming. In the years ahead, the image of a farmer toiling in his field will be outdated. Instead, imagine a team of robots doing the work while the farmer supervises. A whole range of agricultural robots is currently being developed. These robots will be able to handle almost all of the daily chores required to keep a farm productive, from planting and weeding fields to caring for animals. This will leave the farmer free to perform the few chores that robots cannot. With these capabilities, farmers should also be able to produce more crops than ever before.

This guard robot is capable of providing useful information to a building's visitors.

GUARDING THE GUARDS

Most problems with security are a result of human error or untrustworthy workers. Robots could make these issues a thing of the past. They will always follow orders faithfully, making them ideal for the security business. Security robots will one day protect stores, warehouses, prisons, military installations, schools, and much more. Some will be large and obvious, patrolling just like a team of uniformed guards do today. Others will be small and subtle. We are entering the age of nanobots—machines so tiny that they are all but invisible. Coupled with artificial intelligence, these security bots should be able to dramatically reduce everything from home invasions and property theft to acts of terrorism.

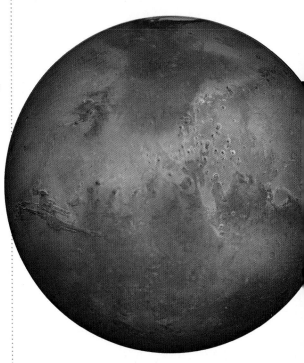

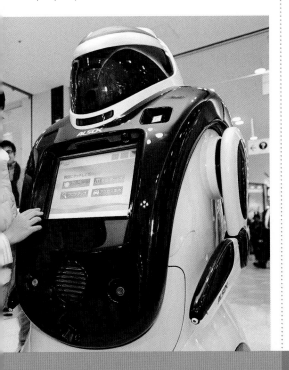

THERE AND BACK AGAIN

Yes, robots have been to Mars already—but the next time they go, it'll be better than ever before. NASA is working on an all-new Mars rover due to launch in 2020. This rover will collect samples of Martian rocks and dirt and package them in containers that a future rover could collect and place on a rocket to be returned to Earth. Those samples could help scientists determine once and for all whether life ever existed on the Red Planet. It could also help them figure out whether or not Mars could support human life. With this information, scientists could begin planning the first crewed flight to Mars!

CAREER STATS

MECHANICAL ENGINEERS

MEDIAN ANNUAL SALARY (2012): $80,580

NUMBER OF JOBS (2012): 258,100

PROJECTED JOB GROWTH, 2012–2022: 5%, slower than average

PROJECTED INCREASE IN JOBS, 2012–2022: 11,600

REQUIRED EDUCATION: Bachelor's degree

LICENSE/CERTIFICATION: May be required for some positions

MECHANICAL ENGINEERING TECHNICIANS

MEDIAN ANNUAL SALARY (2012): $51,980

NUMBER OF JOBS (2012): 47,500

PROJECTED JOB GROWTH, 2012–2022: 5%, slower than average

PROJECTED INCREASE IN JOBS, 2012–2022: 2,200

REQUIRED EDUCATION: Associate's degree or other postsecondary education

LICENSE/CERTIFICATION: May be required for some positions

COMPUTER HARDWARE ENGINEERS

MEDIAN ANNUAL SALARY (2012): $100,920

NUMBER OF JOBS (2012): 83,300

PROJECTED JOB GROWTH, 2012–2022: 7%, slower than average

PROJECTED INCREASE IN JOBS, 2012–2022: 6,200

REQUIRED EDUCATION: Bachelor's degree

LICENSE/CERTIFICATION: May be required for some positions

Figures reported by the United States Bureau of Labor Statistics

RESOURCES

BOOKS

Becker, Helaine. *Zoobots: Wild Robots Inspired by Real Animals.* Tonawanda, NY: Kids Can Press, 2014.

Furstinger, Nancy. *Helper Robots.* Minneapolis: Lerner Publications, 2014.

Furstinger, Nancy. *Robots in Space.* Minneapolis: Lerner Publications, 2014.

Manatt, Kathleen. *Robot Scientist.* North Mankato, MN: Cherry Lake Publishing, 2014.

FACTS FOR NOW

Visit this Scholastic Web site for more information on robotics:
www.factsfornow.scholastic.com
Enter the keyword **Robotics**

GLOSSARY

artificial intelligence (ahr-tuh-FISH-uhl in-TEL-i-juhns) the science of making computers do things that previously needed human intelligence, such as understanding language

automatons (aw-TAH-muh-tahnz) mechanical devices designed to perform a physical function, often one that is repetitive

drone (DROHN) an aircraft without a pilot that is controlled remotely

GPS (GEE PEE ESS) a system of satellites and devices people use to find out where they are or to get directions to a place; GPS is short for "global positioning system"

humanoid (HYOO-muh-noyd) shaped like a human

patent (PAT-uhnt) a legal document giving the inventor of an item the sole right to manufacture or sell it

probes (PROHBZ) tools or devices used to explore or examine something

prosthetic (prahs-THET-ik) artificial and intended to replace a missing part of a body

prototype (PROH-tuh-tipe) the first version of an invention that tests an idea to see if it will work

simulated (SIM-yuh-lay-tid) imitated a real-life situation

INDEX

Page numbers in *italics* indicates illustrations.

INDEX *(CONTINUED)*

ABOUT THE AUTHOR

WIL MARA has been following the development of robotic technology ever since he was given a copy of Joseph Weizenbaum's 1976 landmark book *Computer Power and Human Reason*, which considered the philosophical perils of computer-based artificial intelligence. Wil is the award-winning, best-selling author of more than 150 books, many of which are educational titles for children.